Reflections from the Heart

My Journey to Wholeness Through the Poetic

LANETTA R. ALLEN

Because There's More Publishing | Georgia

Copyright © 2011 by Lanetta R. Allen

All rights reserved. This book is protected under the copyright laws of the United States of America. This book or any portion thereof may not be reproduced or used in any manner whatsoever without the express written permission of the publisher except for the use of brief quotations in a book view.

Unless otherwise noted, scripture quotations are taken from the New King James Version of the Holy Bible.

ISBN: 979-8-9990652-0-9 (Hardback)
ISBN: 979-8-9990652-1-6 (Paperback)

Printed in the United States of America.

Published by:
Because There's More Publishing LLC
PO Box 390163
Snellville, GA 30039
becausetheresmorepublishing.com

Dedication

To the one who taught me to believe...

I dedicate this book of reflections to the One who taught me to believe beyond my own limitations and trust His ability. To embrace my own uniqueness and see the beauty in myself and others. Who showed me what true love looks like. Who made whole, my bruised and wounded heart - once closed, now open to love again, dream again, hope again...The Lord Jesus Christ.

To my wonderful mother and greatest cheerleader, Annie Allen - thank you for your love, support, and sacrifice through the years. You showed me what resiliency looks like.

To my beautiful daughter, Laniecia Davis. You have been my greatest motivation. Thank you for all your hugs, kisses, laughs, and encouraging words. You have shown me love through a child's eyes. Now you are a mother yourself. May your three precious jewels continue to inspire you and shower you with love in abundance.

Acknowledgments
MANY THANKS

It is true that "no man is an island," and I am so glad I didn't have to stand alone in this work.

Thank You, Lord, for using me as a conduit of Your creative, transforming power. I marvel at the thoughts and expressions You have penned through me. You never cease to amaze me. You are a constant source of inspiration and I give You all the glory!

To take what God has placed on the inside of me, pen it to paper, and create this book required the help and support of a host of individuals whom I appreciate and must acknowledge.

To my family, for their overwhelming love and support: Laniecia Davis, Annie Allen, Tangela Allen, Vernon Allen, Chawanda Allen, Regina & Dewitt Johnson, Vickie Mitchell, and a host of uncles, aunts, cousins, nieces, and nephews.

Thank you to the pastors whose leadership played a significant role in shaping my life during the time this book was penned. Thank you, Pastor Joyce Terrell for laying the foundation for prayer. The beginning of these writings started at Oasis. This period marked one of the most turbulent, yet wonderful, times in my life - conversion and trials. I must say that I would not have made it through without prayer and the Word... it is how God kept me sane. Thank you!

Thank you, Bishop Kent and Pastor Diana Branch, for allowing God to use you to cultivate and mentor me through the Word of God. Thank you for your example of excellence in leadership, for embracing the diversity of gifts within your sons and daughters in the gospel, and for giving us a platform to develop and express them. Although some of these writings predate our meeting, it is under your leadership that God blessed me to finish this work.

Thank you to Sabrina & Franklin Westmoreland and Jonathan Miles, for your friendship, support, love, and prayers.

Thank you to Diann Johnson and Loston Fudd for encouraging me in my writings. We may not all speak in the same voice; however, you taught me that my voice is relevant and needs to be heard.

Thank you so much to all who played a role in the fulfillment of this dream. Not only was God with me, but He surrounded me with great people like you and for that I am eternally grateful.

Contents

REFLECTIONS FROM THE HEART

> Come with me on a journey through my heart.

12	**Prologue: Finding My Voice**	
	Indescribable	17
	The Name	20
	Thanksgiving Day	22
	The Greatest Gift	25
	I Marvel	29
	The Sound	30
	Solace	31
	God's Healing Power	31
	The Sacrifice	32
34	**Intermission I: I Am Because He Is**	
	Only Because of You	36
	My Reality	37
	My King	40
	To My Beloved	42
	The Shift	46
	Go!	50
54	**Intermission II: The Road to Promise**	
	Life's Contradictions	56
	The Unfamiliar	61
	Why Not?	65
	A Page from My Journal	69
	The Wait	71
	No Limits	75

	Because You Did It My Way	77
82	**Intermission III: To Know Love, To Be Loved, To Love**	
	Set the Atmosphere	85
	Worship	89
	Intimacy Calls	91
	Psalm of Love and Endearment	93
	My Love Song	95
	My Love Note to God	97
	What is Love?	99
	Your Love Never Dies	104
	The Love of God	106
	The Answer	109
113	**Coming Full Circle**	
	I Am Fierce	117
	You Are Man, You Are Beautiful	121
126	**Epilogue**	
	I Hope You Dance	129

Prologue
FINDING MY VOICE

> My heart is stirred by a noble theme as I recite my verses for the king; my tongue is the pen of a skillful writer.
>
> *Psalm 45:1*

For many years, the ability to express myself verbally eluded me. It seemed as if there was a disconnect. To take the thoughts that were in my head and give voice to them through my mouth was like pulling teeth. So to say the least, speaking wasn't my preferred mode of expression – the gift of gab bypassed me.

However, what was difficult for me to say verbally flowed easier through pen. There was a liberty, a certain freedom that came through writing. It was an outlet – a way to share and let go of what was in my heart. Here, I found my voice.

The reflections contained in this book cover a period in my life marked by great disappointments, hurts and pains, as well as accomplishments and victories. My journey from a place of brokenness to wholeness required that I let go of some things that I harbored and pinned up in my heart over the years. There is an old saying that a closed fist can't receive anything, but neither could my closed and broken heart. It was through these writings, prayer and God's Word that I was able to let go and be made whole.

Be forewarned. You will encounter run-on sentences, fragments, split verbs, made-up words, incorrect grammar and punctuation usage, and more. Why? **Life is rarely a perfect sentence**. There are pauses and interruptions in places that we never expected; and times when we wanted to quit, life demanded that we run-on. My English teachers would probably scold me for what I'm about to say, but for a moment, forget what you were taught in school and listen to my heart.

The common thread woven throughout all of these pieces is God. Each reflection in some way conveys a message about the God whose intense love for me absolutely transformed my life for the better. I learned to trust, love, hope and dream again through relationship with Him. As I reflected on His goodness, I could see the good in others. As I considered His mercy towards me, I could extend mercy to others. As I thought about how He forgave me, I was able to forgive others. The more I came to know Him, the more I came to know myself. The person I am today and still becoming is all because of who God is.

No matter where we are in our walk with Christ, there is always more to experience. I pray that as you read these writings, you too will find yourself yearning to know God more closely and in doing so, not only find your voice, but discover more about who God is and who He has purposed for you to be in Him.

The end of each section presents an opportunity for you to journal your own reflections. Write as He inspires.

Nothing is random in God.

When words seem inadequate, I write still...

Indescribable

A Poet's words cannot describe
the love I feel inside.

The warmth of Your embrace,
the tenderness of Your touch,
the undying, eternal peace of Your presence.

Lord, what expressions can flawlessly portray
You?

What tribute exclusively epitomizes You?
How can we fully return in measure
the depth and richness of Your love shown to us?

No matter what we offer to You,
it still doesn't quite seem enough.

What shall we render, O Lord,
for all your many benefits unto us?
A lifetime of praise
An eternal worship
Submission to Your will
Our lives a living sacrifice to You

What, Oh Lord, shall we give?

An eternity of pure, fluent praise and worship
still pales in the brilliance of
Your immense love for us.

We can never repay You for
Your lovingkindness unto us.

How can we amply convey our love,
appreciation and gratitude to You?
No language in the universe can come close -
nor the most gifted writer's pen,
nor the most anointed worship hymn.

They all fall short of embodying the true essence
of who You are.

How do you begin to describe the God
whose rule expands that of the universe
and all that it encompasses?

Whose very existence and presence
supersede time,
launched and residing in eternity -

Who created all that we see
by the spoken word,
who unveils,
makes known the hidden truths

of this world and the world to come...

Who sees all,
hears all,
knows all,
forever reigning over all.

This feat seems quite impossible to achieve.
Yet it does not discourage
nor inhibit us
from endeavoring to describe the Indescribable.

For His love is just too vast to contain.
His grace unto us, too great not to disclose.
His mercy towards us, too numerous not to share.

His goodness, we must proclaim!
His name, we must praise!
His righteousness,
His holiness -
We must declare!

Our God, we must worship!
We cannot keep silent.
For the very fiber of our being,
the very heart of who we are
is wrapped in Him…
The Indescribable!

The Name

No other name commands -
the respect,
the awe,
the attention of everything
clothed in the universe -
having preeminence over all that is
in the heavens and the earth.

How excellent is Thy Name!

There is no other name
by which man must be saved.

The name of Jesus -
penetrates the depths
of our souls and spirits,
liberating us to fulfill
purpose and destiny in the earth.

How excellent is Thy Name!

No other name is gentle enough
to quiet the cries of a baby's frantic heart -
and powerful enough
to completely subdue and destroy

the works of satan.

How excellent is Thy Name!

No other name exists
in which there is abundance
and richness of life.

The miraculous is manifested.
Salvation abides.
Healings and deliverances transpire -
converting the soul
and making whole.

How excellent is Thy Name!

There is no other name
worthy of praise,
reverence,
and exaltation.

The name of Jesus is -
majestic,
splendid,
magnificent...
bathed and dressed in glory.

How excellent is Thy Name!

Thanksgiving Day

Thanksgiving -
a time of reflection,
to offer our thanks, gratitude, and appreciation
to God for all He has given unto us.

Thank You, Lord, for Your undying love for humanity.
Your love propels and stirs us -
drawing us closer to You
with each passing day.

Thank You, Lord, for forgiving us.
We are no longer condemned
to remain and die in a sinful state.

Because of the redemptive work of the Cross,
and the Blood of Jesus Christ,
we can embrace salvation
and be free from our past regrets and mistakes.

Thank You, Lord, for abundant life -
life not satisfied by human ability,
nor intellect,
nor pacified by material wealth or accolades...

But life that is rich in relationship
and in love with You.

A life full of peace
Wrapped in mercy
Immersed in glory
Shadowed in grace
Victorious in praise
Eternalized in worship

Thank You, Lord, for being my God -
our God.
The God of the heavens and the earth.

Strong in my weakness
Faithful in my unfaithfulness
Uncompromising and unwavering
  in my double-mindedness
Constant in instability.
True and honest in a world of deceit

Dependable and reliable -
always present
to instruct, guide, teach, and comfort me.

Our Healer in sickness
Our Provider in need

Thank You, Lord,
for being my All-in-All -
completely sufficient and entire.

We love You, Lord.
And because of You -
Every day is Thanksgiving Day.

For God so loved the world that He gave His only begotten Son, that whoever believes in Him should not perish but have everlasting life.
John 3:16

The Greatest Gift

This time of year, lights are all aglow.
Community after community, city after city,
are charged with electrifying bliss
that rides on the tails of holiday cheer…

It's Christmas time!

Streets are bustling with cars.
Frazzled shoppers hurry from store to store,
looking to find that right gift
for that special loved one.

Children eagerly anticipate the arrival of
Christmas Day,
to discover the treasures hidden within
beautifully wrapped boxes under the Christmas
tree.

Now it's Christmas Eve…
Night falls, and sleep seems to escape them,
as the clock slowly ticks toward midnight.

Finally, it strikes -
It's Christmas!

Families frantically search for presents
bearing their names.

Utter joy rushes through their souls
as they rip off the wrappings and tear open the boxes,
revealing precious jewels, trinkets, gadgets, toys,
and the like.

Yet, one gift remains -
The greatest gift of all…

Priceless,
immeasurable in the depth of love.

Hidden to those who fail to receive Him,
revealed to the ones who unwrap
and open their hearts to Him.

He is now the treasure our souls seek,
and our spirits soar after.

Who is this awesome, wonderful Gift?

Jesus Christ!

He is the gift that keeps on giving.
He captures your heart and never lets it go.

His touch is amazing,
His love awe-inspiring,
His embrace comforting,
His mercy enduring.

It is a certainty that once Christ is received into our hearts - we are forever changed.

We have access to the Gift
that money can't buy,
nor can the most powerful person
in the world take away:
the gift of eternal life,
through our Lord and Savior, Jesus Christ.

If you haven't already -
unwrap your heart to Jesus,
and He will reveal Himself to you.
Welcome Him into your life
and He will transform you.

Celebrate Jesus!
After all, He is the reason for this season -
The Greatest Gift of All.

The beauty in serving God is that I get to experience life with Him and see it through His lens. There is always more to see.

I Marvel

Jesus, I marvel at You -
Your power,
Your authority,
Your love,
Your majesty.

You are too much for me.
You render me speechless,
You leave me utterly amazed in Your glory.

Jesus, I marvel at You.

The Sound

The world is composed of many instruments,
bearing a mirage of sounds.

However, there is a distinctive sound
that bears Your mark.

You gather the instruments from the uttermost
parts of the earth - those bearing Your name,
Your insignia upon their foreheads.

As a masterful and skilled composer,
You effortlessly conduct the chosen instruments,
creating a symphonious, harmonious sound:
The sound of one, unified in spirit -
Your Body – The Body of Christ.

Solace

The Lord gathers us into His arms
and comforts the hearts of His people.
Enfolding us in His love,
draping us in His peace.

God's Healing Power

The healing power of God is unceasing.
It never wanes, nor diminishes in strength.

Like the mouths of the great seas -
on a continuum, opening to draw in the
invigorating rivers of life

God's healing power continuously flows,
granting life and wholeness
to all who partake of its streams.

The Sacrifice

No sacrifice was too great.
No burden too hard to bear.

He poured Himself out as a drink offering,
an atonement for my sins,
redeeming my soul.

Now, through the power of His blood,
I am free and made whole.

REFLECTION

Intermission I

I AM BECAUSE HE IS

> For in Him we live and move and have our being, as also some of your own poets have said, 'For we are also His offspring.' Therefore, since we are the offspring of God, we ought not to think that the Divine Nature is like gold or silver or stone, something shaped by art and man's devising.
>
> *Acts 17:28-29*

God, in His omniscience, saw the frailty of my flesh - the good, the bad, and the ugly. Yet He still chose to create me, to love me, and to extend His grace and mercy to me! No prerequisites had to be met. My existence was deemed enough. He loved and still loves me with an everlasting love.

I was always important to God. You see, He didn't abandon me. I abandoned Him. But the depth of His love for me awakened a need to respond to Him -
to respond to His suffering,
to respond to His sacrifice,
to respond to His cry for reconciliation with me.

I've come to realize that the more I understand who God is and who I am to God - the value He sees and has placed on my life - the more I gravitate toward Him, the more I believe and trust Him, the more I love Him, and the more I long to fulfill the purpose for which He created me:

To bring Him Glory!

Only Because of You

I live,
breathe,
move -
only because of You.

I have peace, hope
joy and strength -
only because of You.

I have freedom to worship,
liberty to praise,
power to overcome -
only because of You.

My soul is redeemed;
I am now a child of the King!
Life eternal is my reward.

Your glory - my sanctuary.
Your presence - my dwelling place.
Only because of You.

Thank You, Lord, for being You.
For now, I am complete…
Only because of You.

My Reality

You are my reality, O Lord.
Though unseen with the natural eye,
You are most certainly real.

The very fact that I awake every morn
declares Your existence.

When I need or desire
the safety of a Father's protective embrace,
the security and peacefulness of
Your amazing Presence overshadows me.

Your touch is like no other.
It quickens, yet comforts.
It awakens, yet stills.
It sets ablaze, yet dissipates -
wonderful beyond compare.

Intimacy with You is like the consummation
of cascading waterfalls:

Vibrant and alive,
Sweet and potent,
Beautiful and awe-inspiring,
Calming and jubilant,

Enlightening and illuminating -
and much more than human vernacular can describe.

Lord, Your voice is distinctive,
resonating out of Glory
into my reality.

Your voice is glorious and strong -
inciting response,
yet commanding silence.

You supersede awesome.
You eclipse magnificence.

You are my reality.
My God, You shall forever be.

I love and thank You, Jesus.
For now, I know that
my reality rests in You -

not in this world,
not in other people,
not even in me.

Thank You again
for being my reality.

But the Lord is the true God; He is the living God and the everlasting King.
Jeremiah 10:10

My King

The vastness of the universe -
creation displayed brilliantly for all mankind.

Who can deny Your existence?
Who can deny Your glory?

You are
Who was, and is, and is to come.
The First and the Last,
The Beginning and the End,
The Eternal Father,
The preeminent, everlasting King,
Our sovereign Lord
who alone reigns supreme.

There is no one like You, Lord -
sweet Savior, sweet King.

My soul rejoices in You.
To know You is my cry.
To commune with You is my desire.
To love You more is my plea.

You have captured my heart, O Lord.
You have stirred my very soul.

All that is and is to come,
All that I am and am to be -
I give to You, my King.

My heart leaps when He speaks...

To My Beloved

You are My Beloved, My Chosen -
the expression of My uniqueness,
the quintessence of My beauty.

When I fashioned you,
I did so with forethought and purpose.
You were not a mishap
or an unexpected interruption in My plan.

I've always known about you.

You were wonderfully and fearfully made
for My pleasure.

Love interwove every intricate detail -
from the arch in your brow to the gait in your step,
from the look in your eye to your infatuating smile.
You were My design.

With My hands, I shaped you.
With My Spirit, I quickened you.

As My breath entered your earth,
you became a living soul…

With the capacity:
to love,
to hear,
to speak,
to see,
to taste,
to touch -

To dream dreams,
to believe - yes, I say, to believe!

To believe that all things are possible,
no matter what comes your way.

To believe that you are coming out on top,
despite what you hear or face.

To believe you are more than a conqueror,
because you have God on your side.

To believe My Word - because I cannot lie.

To believe that with My stripes you are healed,
even when doctors have given up hope.

To believe your children shall be saved and set free,
though the enemy looks like he's holding the rope.

To believe that the same God
who made you out of dirt -
can take the dirt in your life
and turn it into a work of art
for His glory.

To believe that the same God who said
"Let there be" to nothing - and there was -
can speak to your nothingness
and cause it to manifest what He has spoken.

To believe.
To believe again.
To keep on believing…

until the purpose for which I created you
is no longer hidden in earth.

But, the treasure housed in this earthen vessel
is free to move,
to do, and
to propel you to your destiny.

**Therefore,
if anyone
is in Christ,
he is a new creation;
old things
have passed away;
behold all things
have become new.**

2 Corinthians 5:17

The Shift

As I look through the window
of my past,
I see what I used to be.

My past failures,
regrets,
mistakes.

The accomplishments,
hurt,
pain.

The things lost
and the things gained.

But what was is no longer what is.
And the place that I was in,
I am no longer.

A shift has occurred.
I've been moved -
transported to a place beyond time,
a place of unlimited worship,
God's eternal dwelling,
the place where He is.

Here…
There are no distractions,
no confusion,
no restlessness.

There is total calmness.
Peacefulness.

Yet one only has to be here for a moment to realize
that it is also saturated with
immense power and strength.

I find myself in awe of His glory,
captivated by the intensity of His presence.

I ask God,
"Why am I here?"
For I can still look through the window of my past
and see what I was.

But in a flash -
the window closes.

And the picture of who I was
vanishes into oblivion.

What remains is who I am now.
Who I am in Eternity.

Who God sees me as,
And not how I see myself.

His completed work.

His vessel of majesty.
His vessel of honor.
His vessel of strength.
His vessel of beauty.

He sees His image,
a reflection of His likeness.
He sees Himself,
looking back at Him.

At that very moment, I realize:
This place, this shift,
is not about me.
It's not even about you.

It's not about the mere acquisition
of more cars,
more houses,
more land,
or more money.

This place is all about Jesus!

In this shift -
we decrease,
so He can increase.

We die to our will
to manifest His will.

We show forth who God is,
not who we are, to:
the dying
the hurting
the lost
the despondent
the tormented
the bound
and the free.

> **Then the master said to the servant, 'Go out into the highways and hedges, and compel them to come in, that my house may be filled.**
> *Luke 14:23*

GO!

Where are the called-out ones?
The ones I've separated unto Myself to be:
A chosen generation
A royal priesthood
A holy nation

You know…
The ones that I have redeemed.

Those who were once enslaved in sin,
but are no longer.

They are now free -
Free to serve Me,
Free to love Me,
Free to worship Me.

You know them…
That's you!

You are the called-out ones -
the ones whom I have called
out of darkness
into My marvelous light.

Now you are the light
that I've placed in this world
to glorify and point the way to Me.

Now GO!

GO, compel men to come.

GO until those who are bound are set free.

GO until those without hope experience the Hope
that is within Me.

GO until the burdened find rest in Me.

GO until men come running, saying:
"What must I do to be saved?"

GO until strongholds are broken,
yokes are destroyed,
broken hearts are mended,
diseased bodies are healed,
and backsliders restored.

GO, proclaim My Word
to every nation,
every ethnicity,
in every tongue.

GO, reveal the Word that became flesh for you.

GO, reveal My Glory.

Speak, Lord!

Then I heard the voice of the Lord saying, "Whom shall I send? And who will go for us?" And I said, "Here am I. Send me!"
Isaiah 6:8

REFLECTION

Intermission II

THE ROAD TO PROMISE

> Jesus answered, "I am the way and the truth and the life."
> *John 14:6*

At some point in time, all of us have reached - or will reach - a fork in the road: the decisive moment when we must choose whether to do it God's way or our own.

God's way is always the best way.

You see, there are certain blessings that only come through submission to God's will.

There are certain promises that are only realized through obedience to His Word.

The strong start…
The momentum to continue strong…
The ability to finish strong…
All come through doing it God's way.

His way is the road to promise.

Life's Contradictions

What happens when your desires
are no longer your desires?

When your goals no longer matter?
They seem obsolete now,
in the grand scheme of things.

What happens when receiving the thing
you thought you wanted
turns out to be a heavy burden?

What happens after the idol
you set up in your heart
falls off its pedestal,
crumbling in a useless heap to the ground?

The trappings of its lure
no longer mesmerize you.
God and His will now captivate you.

It is sad -
how one can work so hard toward a goal,
come to the end
and realize:
this isn't it.

You don't even want it.
It's not at all how you imagined.

You allowed your relationship with God to suffer.
Leanness filled your spirit -
all in pursuit of a prize
you can care less about.

So much time…
wasted.

Now you grasp that God
is more important
than any goal you set out to accomplish.

Your focus is once again upon your God -
To abide in His presence,
To appear before your Father
openly and boldly,
doing His will.

His desires are now becoming your desires.
You are committing your ways to Him,
so He can establish your thoughts.
All you long to do is delight Him.

Finding yourself at a crossroads,
you ask the question:

"Do I pursue my will or God's will?"

Everyone is watching you.
They are expecting you
to accomplish this great milestone in your life.

They are waiting to see
if you will fulfill the five-year plan
you mapped out for yourself.

You considered most variables
and possible outliers -
however,
you failed to consider
the most important person of all: God.

Now you realize
that your plan for your life
contradicts God's will for you.

You need to regroup.
Let some things go.
Let some people go.

But what will they say?

"You're giving up this for what? What is wrong with you?"

"God says what? You're mistaken."
"Just sleep on it...you'll see things differently in the morning."

The enemy bombards your mind
with all kinds of scenarios -
to instill fear and doubt,
based on what you think someone may say.

But the thoughts
do not constitute reality.

Even if public opinion is contrary -
whose opinion means more to you?
God's or man's?

Choose for yourselves this day whom you will serve...
Joshua 24:15

For I know the thoughts that I think toward you, says the Lord, thoughts of peace and not of evil, to give you a future and a hope.
Jeremiah 29:11

The Unfamiliar

I've come into unfamiliar territory -
a place I've never been before.

It requires my heart to be sensitive,
my hearing to be sharper than ever
before.

To seek God early
and often.
To know His voice.

It's the unfamiliar -
strange,
yet wonderful,
all at the same time.

Every step deliberate,
on a course
whose designer is Divine.

I sense the pull...
the pull toward destiny.
It's knocking at my heart's door -
the beats becoming louder,
a sound too powerful to ignore.

So I continue on this path -
the one God has chosen for me:
the unfamiliar.

It's the place where I learn
more about who He is
and who I am.

Where I realize just how much
I need Him
and must rely on Him.

His Spirit is my compass
guiding and directing me.
His Word,
my only roadmap.

This is the place where I learn
to trust God with my whole heart,
to walk by faith,
not by sight.

I'm moving forward -
forward past what I have known,
past what I have experienced,
past my comfort zone -

The places I had mastered navigating on
my own.

Deeper into the unfamiliar,
to the More that God has for me.

Yes, the More...
all that He has purposed
for His glory.

As deep cries out to deep,
I'm consumed by the presence
of God's peace -
peace in knowing that
He knows the way I must go
and is ever with me.

So I continue onward -
forward,
forward still.

Through the unfamiliar,
I must go.
It is God's will.

God can do it for you too. You've believed God for others. Now, it's time to believe God for yourself!

Why Not?

Why not believe God for those things
which some say are impossible?

Isn't He still a miraculous,
wonder-working God?
Why not put all your faith and
confidence in the Lord?

Isn't He still able to deliver?
Isn't He a covenant-keeping God?
Isn't His Word true?

Are all these truths nothing more than
clichés to us?
They sound good to say.
They appease us for the moment.
They give the appearance of trust in a
sovereign God...

But do we really trust Him?
Do we really believe?

Now is the time
to believe God with our whole heart -
To take a stand for Truth.

To rest on God's promises.
To endure the trying of our faith!

People may think you're crazy
because they don't see
what God has privileged you to see.

Be strong in the Lord.
Trust and believe.
Endure the trying of your faith.

Even when the promise
appears to be slipping away.
Even when the circumstances
seem to have gotten worse instead of
better -

Hold on to the Word of God.
Endure the trying of your faith.

At times, you question God:

"Is this really Your will?"

You even question your own thinking:

"Is this faith or foolishness?"

This thing defies human logic
and reasoning.
But even in your questioning,
a secret hope still remains.

The Word of God grips you.
Sometimes, you don't even understand
yourself -
You just know you can't let go now.

God won't let you give up.
He won't let you quit.

So just be still,
and know that the Lord, He is God.

Endure the trying of your faith.

Then one day, you awake and ask
yourself:

Why not?

Why can't I be a recipient of God's
promises?

Why not expect God
to work a miracle in my life?

Why can't my test
testify of His power
and glorify Him?

All will know that God did it -
for many have said (including you):

This thing will take God.

So…

Why not now?
Why not you?

Yes - you.
Yes - now.
Yes - with God.

No more wondering…
Just believe!

It is impossible for God to lie.
Hebrews 6:18

A Page from My Journal
Delay is Not Denial

"We're having a good day!" I've felt that in my spirit since I awoke this morning. But those words still don't quite convey what I really feel. You see, it's not just about this day. Personally, I sense that things are starting to fall into place for me. Those things I've been waiting on - I will begin to see. It's part of starting and finishing this new year strong.

Although the journey has been arduous at times, God has remained faithful. Even when I questioned His promises, He didn't change His mind. Personally, most times - if not all - a period of waiting has preceded the receipt of God's promise. And there were times when I questioned why. Why couldn't I be one of those who received a word and saw it come to pass immediately? Then I was reminded of Hebrews 10:36–38, which reads in the Amplified version: "For you have need of steadfast patience and endurance, so that you may perform and fully accomplish the will of God, and thus receive and carry away [and enjoy to the full] what is promised. For still a little while (a very little while), and the Coming One will come and He will not delay. But the just shall live by faith…" Selah.

My wait wasn't a denial of God's promise, but a time to work out and perfect some things in my life. It's like a mother pregnant with child. Conception and delivery do not transpire simultaneously. There's a period of gestation that is needed for the growth and development of both mother and child. Despite the morning sickness, the stretching, the added weight, and more, a mother knows that the promise coming is far greater than what she is currently experiencing. Thus, she endures to the end. So, we must do the same.

Having said that, I'm the first to admit that it's not always easy. But God, who is faithful, extends His grace and mercy to us along the way so we can endure. The work that has been and is being produced in my life far exceeds the momentary discomfort and pain I've encountered. When you've waited on God and endured the trying of your faith in the process, it makes the receipt of the promises that much sweeter - at least for me. There's a greater level of appreciation, gratefulness, and joy that comes with the fulfillment of God's Word in your life.

So be encouraged to run on and endure to the end. So you too can go on and apprehend what God has promised you!

The Wait
In Between the Promise and the Performance

At some point in time, you will find yourself in the in-between place - the place between the promise and the performance of God's Word. Many of us are excited when we receive a word from God. We shout, we dance, we praise, and we believe God in that moment to do exactly what He said He would do. And the truth of the matter is, He will. However, most times, the promise isn't manifested instantaneously. There's this in-between place, called WAIT. Below are a few nuggets on how to deal with the wait.

WAIT is defined as "the time during which some action is awaited." The problem isn't the place or the time, but our perception of the place. When we fail to understand that WAIT has purpose, we can shift from watching and expecting God to move, to growing frustrated that He hasn't done it yet.

So our first nugget of encouragement is this: WAIT has purpose.

From a spiritual aspect, waiting can produce patience, endurance, steadfastness, and help to mature and develop our faith (Hebrews 10:36, James 1:4).

From a natural standpoint, waiting gives us time to get in position to receive the promise. If God promised you advancement in your career, use this time to improve your skill sets. If God promised you a spouse, use this time to prepare yourself for that relationship. If God promised you a house, use this time to work on your credit and save money.

God hasn't forgotten the promise. It could be that He's just waiting on us to get in the right position to receive it. In addition to knowing that WAIT has purpose, we must also call to remembrance what God said and who He is.

The first part of this nugget deals with what God said.

His Word acts as a safety net or buffer. So when doubt comes, we are able to silence the doubt with the Word. Instead of doubting God's Word, doubt the doubt that came to steal it.

Secondly, calling to remembrance what God said helps us stay focused.

When we're focused, we're less likely to settle for a substitute out of frustration or fall for a counterfeit out of desperation. Instead, we press on to apprehend the true promise.

The final part of this nugget is to remember who God is.

It's easier to hold on to the promise when you know and understand the fidelity of the One who made it. *"God is not a man, that He should lie, nor a son of man, that He should change His mind. Does He speak and then not act? Does He promise and not fulfill?"* (Numbers 23:19, NIV). No - all of God's promises are yes and amen (2 Corinthians 1:20).

And finally, because I understand that the wait has purpose, and I've recalled His Word and who He is, I can praise Him right here in my in-between place.

In-between is a middle point - not the beginning and not the end. The WAIT is just our middle. He gave us the beginning - His promise - and He will give us the end - the performance.

So be encouraged: God will do what He said He would do!

For with God nothing shall be impossible.
Luke 1:37

No Limits

Don't you know who I Am?
I Am the Almighty God.

There is nothing impossible for Me.
There is nothing too hard for Me.
I specialize in the hard thing.

I Am that same God -
Who spoke to the darkness hovering over the earth
and said, Let there be…
and light came forth.

I Am that same God -
Who formed man from the dust of the ground,
blew into him the breath of life,
and he became a living soul.

If only you could grasp the depth of My power…

Don't constrain Me.
Don't box Me in.

Let Me be who I want to be in you.

Release Me from your:

I can't.
It won't happen.
It's been too long.

I'm bigger than that!

Don't limit Me.
Free Me.
Take the limits off.

No Limits!

> **Now unto Him who is able to do exceedingly abundantly above all that we ask or think, according to the power that works in us...**
> *Ephesians 3:20*

Because You Did It My Way

The wait was long, I know -
and at times, hard to comprehend.
But you said, "Nevertheless, Lord - not my will,
but His."

You looked to the right…
the answer was not there.
To the left… still no reply.
Then you looked up to Me,
and I guided you with My eye.

You said, "Lord, I don't understand,"
yet you followed hard after Me still.
You learned to rest in the truth
that I know all things
and My peace in you I instilled.

You see,
you could've given up -
but you grabbed hold of My words:
"You're finishing strong."

You could've caved in under pressure,
but you remembered My words:
"The best is yet to come."

You gave it all you got
and shot your best shot.
You prepared yourself
and got in position to receive My favor.

You postured yourself
and prophesied the words I spoke over your situation -
dry places,
dead places,
deserts,
parched paths in the wilderness.

But My Word gave you hope
to expect waters and revitalization.

You embraced your favored future
and declared a strong start.

You partnered with Me in My work -
humanity and divinity working hand in hand.
Vision.
Kingdom purpose.
Strategy to impart.

Your faith in action -
you sharpened your craft.
You took My direction

and applied motion.

Thus:
Progression.
Unlimited possibilities.
The destination now in sight.

You consecrated and submitted yourself to Me,
and thus are able to experience the good part -
Double grace.
Double favor.
Wholeness.
Perfection.
Completed cycles for start.

You delighted yourself in Me,
and committed your way unto Me,
Thus, the hidden desires I have not withheld -
but I granted that which was in the heart.

When people ask, "How you made it?"
tell them I said:

"Because you did it My way."

You heeded My Word -
trusted and obeyed.
You sought My will and not your own.

Your desire to please Me -
greater than your desire to please self.
You wanted it My way, above all else.

When they ask you,
"What's your secret?"
tell them:

"It's nothing deep.
You simply said yes
and surrendered at My feet."

So when you come out on top,
and see your promises come to pass,
and they ask,
"How can this be?"

Tell them I said:

"Because you did it My way -
you followed Me."

Trust God to lead, direct, and guide you. He knows the way.

REFLECTION

Intermission III

TO KNOW LOVE, TO BE LOVED, TO LOVE

> He brought me to the banqueting house, and his banner over me was love.
> *Song of Solomon 2:4*

It is natural for a human being to want to know love, to be loved, and to love. It's part of our makeup, considering that the God who is Love created us. There are three kinds of love: Eros, Philia, and Agape.

Eros is sensual or sexual love - the love between a man and a woman who find themselves yearning for one another. From the warm, fuzzy feelings to the intense passions that arise from "falling in love," this love is often considered the "ultimate experience."

Philia is the kind of love shared between family and friends.

Agape is God's love for us. It is freely given - unconditional and unchanging. All we have to do is receive God's love (John 3:16).

Some people spend their whole lifetime looking for someone to love them and, in their busy search, overlook the love that has always been there, right in front of them: Agape love. God's love is the foundation upon which the other two loves should thrive. If you notice, Eros and Philia are subject to human emotions and thus change. God's love is the only type of love that remains the same. When Eros or Philia fail you, God's love is there to pick up the broken pieces and make you whole again. There is no greater love.

The following poems are a reflection of the love I have received and experienced with God. They were birthed out of a place of worship and praise for my God. You see, my relationship with Him is personal.

He's not a distant being, but a personal God whose desire is for us to know, enjoy, and glorify Him. It is through His love that I have come to love and appreciate others and myself.

The love of God moves me.

Set the Atmosphere
The Power of Praise & Worship

In the beginning, the Word of God tells us that
God created the Heaven and the Earth.
And the earth was without form and void, and
darkness was upon the face of the deep.

Before God said, *"Let there be..."*
The Spirit of God had to move upon the face of the
waters.

That which was a wasteland,
desolate and empty,
had to become conducive for God's move.

So the Spirit of God hovered, incubated over -
like a mother hen over her eggs -
until it was ready to hatch,
to bring forth,
to birth that which God had purposed and was
about to speak.

Now, when the time of gestation was fulfilled,
and the time of delivery had come,
God spoke:

"Let there be..."
And there was.

He said, *"Let them produce after their own kind."*
And they did.

And it was good in His eyes.

Now we fast-forward to our time…

We come with spiritual cups to be filled,
wanting to experience:
The miraculous of God
The power of God
The Presence
The Shekinah Glory of God

But as it was in the days of old, so it is today:
The atmosphere must be conducive for God's move.

So, we enter His gates with thanksgiving,
and His courts with praise.

We come before His presence rejoicing,
and blessing His holy name.

We bestow words of adoration like…

You're Wonderful
Awesome
Mighty
Splendid
Glorious
Holy!

And as we worship,
And as we praise -

God inhabits.
He dwells.
His Glory fills the temple.

And we become immersed in His Presence.

That which was empty becomes full.
That which was broken becomes whole.
That which was bound is set free.

You see...

Your deliverance can be wrapped
in your next Hallelujah.
Your breakthrough, in your next dance.
Your miracle, in the lifting of your hands.

So, I ask you: What atmosphere will you create?

God is Spirit, and those who worship Him must worship in spirit and truth.
John 4:24

Worship

When I think of worship,
the ocean comes into view.

Soft, gentle breezes
blow upon the landscape of our souls,
rippling and inciting
the waters of our spirit -
cresting into waves
of beautiful, intimate worship
to our Lord.

We exhale volumes
of unadulterated truths,
arising from deeply entrenched wells
within our spirits

Speaking of Your love
and our love for You.
Truths of Your Majesty,
Your Holiness,
and Power.

This is between You and Your Beloved...
those who worship You
in spirit and in truth.

**Love is calling...
Will you answer?**

Intimacy Calls

When you consider the marital relationship
and the intimacy experienced
between a husband and a wife -

one may conclude that making love
is a natural, explosive reaction
to myriad meaningful moments
shared between the two.

Intimacy goes beyond physicality.

Intimacy says:
I want to be with you.
I just want to be in your presence.
I just want to hear your voice.
I just want to commune with you.
I just want to know what is on your heart.
I just want to be close to you.
I just want to please you.

Intimacy is not an isolated event or experience.
It is found in the daily interactions
and expressions of love and commitment
to one another.

It's the touching of one's heart
and the fulfilling of one's love language.

Intimacy calls -
but only those sensitive enough to hear,
and hungry enough to answer,
will come near.

God is calling us
to a greater level of intimacy in Him.
He desires to commune with us daily.

Wonderful, intimate moments
climaxed in the secret place
of the Most High God.

God is our Husbandman,
beckoning His bride to come near...

Will you answer?

Yes, I have loved you with an everlasting love; Therefore with lovingkindness I have drawn you.
Jeremiah 31:3

Psalm of Love and Endearment

You have captured my heart, O Lord.
My soul shall rejoice in You forever.

You have been my strength,
my sweet song in the midnight.

Your Glory has encompassed me.
Your love has enthralled me, O God -
the God of my salvation.

Oh, how I love Thee, O Lord,
my sovereign King.

You alone have kept me
from the desires of my enemies.
You have hedged me about
and secured my deliverance.

O God,
You have been my peace in the midst of turmoil,
my contentment in the wilderness,
my joy in sorrow,
and my healing in pain.

O Lord, how I love Thee.

How wonderful is Your Name.
Your praise shall forever flow from my lips.

My arms outstretched to You,
my body bowed before You -
You alone are the focus
of my worship and adoration.

Oh, how I love Thee, O Lord!
Oh, how I love Thee!

You shall love the Lord your God with all your heart, with all your soul, and with all your strength.
Deuteronomy 6:5

My Love Song

My soul loves You.
She aches and yearns deeply for You.

You alone can quench her thirst.
You alone can satiate her desire.

You alone, O Lord,
are the One who can raise her to new heights
take her on journeys - she couldn't even fathom
to think or dream about.

You are:
the well that never runs dry,
the light that is inextinguishable,
the rose that forever blooms,
the sweet fragrance that never wanes -

lingering upon the recesses
of my mind,
my soul,
and spirit.

You are the One –
she, my soul, loves.
I love You, Jesus.

My soul yearns, even faints, for the courts of the LORD; my heart and my flesh cry out for the living God.
Psalm 84:2

My Love Note to God

Thank You, my beautiful Father, for this moment in time with You - for Your magnificent presence and consuming love. You always leave me in awe of You. You are breathtaking.

Thank You for counting me worthy of communion with You, for inviting me into a love relationship with You. You have captivated my heart and captured my thoughts. You are my everything.

Every encounter with You is unique and always comes at a time when I need You most. Thank You for continual revelations of Your Is-ness, Your awesomeness, love, and power.

Through every experience, I've come to know You as my Father, my very Best Friend, Lover of my Soul, Sustainer, Provider, Healer, Deliverer and more.

You have taught me to love again, to hope again, and to dream again. Yes, you!

Thank You for intimate moments of worship that bridge the gap between time and eternity.

As long as You're inviting, I'm responding… with worship to You.

Love You much!

My heart has heard you say, "Come and talk with me." And my heart responds, "Lord, I am coming."
Psalm 27:8 NLT

What is Love?

Love endures.
It is not fleeting,
drifting with the currents
or tossed about in the wind.

In the midst of turmoil and chaos,
Love perseveres and prevails.

Love is pure...
Love loves in spite of.
Love loves regardless of.
Love loves in the sea of.
Love loves without contingencies.

Love is merciful.
Love does not seek to place our heads on the chopping block
every time we make a mistake.
Love seeks to draw us back to Him -
to bring us to a place of repentance.
Love opens His arms, calling us home to Him.
Love embraces us,
while correcting us in love.

Love forgives.

The heart of Love is free from bitterness and strife.
Love's heart refuses to hold grudges
or keep records of wrongs.
Love buries the past.

Love says,
"It's who you are now that matters."
Love says,
"Your best days are ahead of you."

Love liberates and resurrects,
breathing life into you!

Love unites.
Love never discredits or slanders
in order to elevate self.

Love never manipulates or divides
to win others to His side.
Love never kills for self-gain.

Love builds up others around Him -
seeking to help others
achieve success,
realize dreams,
walk in purpose,
and fulfill destiny.

Love humbles.
Love woos others by
displaying, walking, and living in love.

Love is not puffed up or arrogant,
nor jealous or envious of what others have.

Love celebrates.
Love treasures and cherishes
the gifts in each of us,
realizing that each gift, operating at its optimum,
benefits all and everyone gains.

Love never fails.
For God is Love.

Who can love like this?
Somewhere along the way,
we have all fallen short.

One concludes that perfection in true love
is only obtainable
if the Spirit of God is reigning
and continuously at work in you.

Oh, how wonderful it is
to experience God's love.

It is unmatched in its fervency and intensity.
The love of God challenges and stimulates.

Love drives us to cry out
for a heart like His -
birthing in us the desire
to love as passionately as Him.

Love explodes within us a longing
to abide in His presence,
to dwell in His Holy Hill,
until our reflection resembles His.

Love brings you to a place of complete surrender,
a dying to self-will.

A paradigm shift emerges -
the old way of thinking,
the old way of doing
succumbs to Love.

Now your whole focus is doing Love's will.
All you want to do is please Love.
To forever remain
and rest in the Presence of Love.

Who wouldn't love Love?
Who wouldn't want to be loved by Love?

Love, we open our hearts to You.
We welcome You.

Come and dwell with us.
Make Your abode with us.
Stretch out in us.
Have Your way in us.
Be glorified in and through us.

Love us as only You can.

As You love us,
we will love You -
and one another.

Expressing love.
Embracing love.
Living in love - with You.

I'm in love with Jesus.

Your Love Never Dies

Your love never dies.
Unlike the flower that fades and withers away,
Your love remains.

Your love breathes.
It's life to the soul of man that receives it,
strength to those who are weak.

Your love never dies.

Even in our sin,
Your love drew us.
When we fell short,
Your love wooed us.
Once fearful and afraid,
Your love perfected us.

Your love never dies.

Your love awaits us -
eager to embrace us,
to heal all hurt and pain,
to erase all guilt and shame.

Your love never dies.

However,
Your love is never to be mistaken for weakness.
For though You love the souls of men,
You truly do hate the acts and practices of sin.

You showed Your love for all to see
on the Cross of Calvary,
by which we can be delivered
and set free from the penalty of sin,
and take hold of the love
You have bestowed upon all men.

Yet it is up to us
to accept Your gift of salvation,
to surrender at Your throne,
with a yielded heart -
obey Your commands,
do Your will,
and grow in Your love...

Your love that never dies.

The Love of God

Your love surpasses
the depths of the deepest ocean.

Your love eclipses
the expansiveness of the universe.

Your love shines brighter than
the compilation of a million suns.

Your love reflects light
even as the moon -
bringing illumination
to the darkest of hearts.

Your love is as fine wine:
as we age in You,
it only becomes sweeter
and more valuable over time.

As waves crash against the shorelines,
breaking them down
in intensity, power, and strength -
so does Your love
to the stoniest heart.

We melt
under the fervency of Your love for us.

Your love is real and tangible.
We see it, hear it,
and experience it each day:

The breath that we breathe
The food that we eat
The shelter we call home
The healing of our bodies
The renewing of our minds
The restoring of our families
The salvation offered to mankind

Your love is:
Pure in its formality
Rare in its potency

Your love is simply divine.

From courtship to covenant...

The Answer

You are my Husbandman,
my Beloved, in whom I cherish -
the One in whom my heart trusts
and my confidence solely lies.

You are my resting place,
my sanctuary,
my comfort and peace.

From the moment You entered my life,
I knew You were the missing link
that made my life complete.

You filled every void,
every place of emptiness and loneliness.
You took my frailty
and sculpted a vessel of honor -
for Your glory alone.

My life was meaningless without You.
You gave me purpose.

Where darkness once dwelt,
You illuminated with the light of Your love.
Where life once seemed routine and mundane,

emerged vibrancy and vitality.
You are my very best friend!
You know me intimately
and You still love me…
Wow.

You are the one true constant -
through the ups and downs,
tears and frowns,
joys and pain,
laughter and rain -
You remained.

There is liberty with and in You.
I am free to be me.
There is no need to pretend or hide.
I am completely safe and secure with You.

You proved Your love for me
on the Cross of Calvary -
giving Your life, shedding Your blood,
to redeem a sinner such was me.

I have no reason to doubt
Your fidelity,
Your Word.

Therefore, Lord,
I willingly submit my life to You;
vowing to always love and cherish You.
To seek You first in all that I do,
and should I miss the mark,
be quick to repent and seek after You still.

I pray that my life, in measure,
gives back to You what You have
so graciously and freely given to me.

Lord, I love You.
And with all my heart, I say...
I do.

It was a long engagement, but I finally said, "I do." Thank You, Lord, for not giving up on me!

REFLECTION

Coming Full Circle

I'M LOVING ME

> Jesus replied: "Love the Lord your God with all your heart and with all your soul and with all your mind." This is the first and greatest commandment. And the second is like it: "Love your neighbor as yourself."
> *Matthew 22:38-39*

For me, growing in my love for God had a direct impact on my love for myself and others. It is because of His love that I am now able to fulfill the greatest two commandments - those that sum up the ten commandments given to Moses.

Before I can love my neighbor properly, I have to love myself properly.

What does loving myself look like? It means learning to care for my body, guard my peace, and protect my time. It looks like setting healthy boundaries, embracing my worth, and refusing to settle for less than what God intended for me. Loving myself is heart alignment with how God sees me.

The next two pieces focus on loving oneself.

These writings are notably different from the earlier reflections. They carry a little more attitude and spunk! Each one is spoken from a place of confidence - rooted in knowing who you are and valuing yourself as a woman or man of God. Both celebrate God's work in us and the visible transformation now seen by others.

"I Am Fierce" was written for me and my sisters. In this context, fierce means "of superior and exceptional quality."

I call it my coming full circle piece.

It celebrates who I am as a woman and who I'm still becoming. Having dealt with low self-esteem and insecurities, it's liberating to now be in a place where I love me, where I can celebrate not only what God is doing in my life, but in the lives of the women and men around me.

"You Are Man, You Are Beautiful" is an affirming and encouraging piece for my brothers. Your transformation isn't going unnoticed. We see and celebrate the work that God is doing in you. Keep moving forward, my brothers!

I will
praise You,
for I am
fearfully and
wonderfully
made;
Marvelous are
Your works,
And that my soul
knows very well.
Psalm 139:14

I Am Fierce

I am fierce.
I am woman.
Strong.
Determined.

Ain't no little bugs gonna stop me!
Ain't listening to no lies -
my Father has already told me I'm a prize.
wonderfully and fearfully made am I.

I am fierce.
I am woman.
That's me.

From my head to my toes,
even to my little belly rolls.
Yeah, I said it… don't matter.
My Father's loving me
and I'm loving me.

Ain't minding the haters.
Ain't concerned about the spectators.
I am who I am -
loving what God is doing in me.

This transformation is a God thing -
worth celebrating, even if it's just me.
I'll praise Him,
I'll worship Him,
I'll bless Him and say,
"Thank You, Lord, for the work You're
manifesting through me."

I am fierce.
I am woman.
That's me.

Make no apologies
for being who God created me to be:

Blood-washed.
Holy.
Acceptable.

Living the life of a Christian,
a Christ-like woman of God,
set apart to bring Him pleasure and glory.

That's me.

Peculiar.
Beautiful.
Breathing through the breath He blew into me.

I am fierce.
I am woman.
That's me.

I know my value.
I know my worth.
Ain't casting my pearls before swine,
nor giving my body to no man that's not mine -
my husband, that is.

I know who I am.
My Father validates and affirms me daily.
I look my own self in the mirror and say,

"Girl, you look fine today… you are fierce."

I laugh at my own jokes.
Pat my own self on the back.
And take time to tell another sister,

"You're beautiful."

Because I'm fierce like that.

Not haughty.
Not arrogant.
Not conceited.
Not self-inflated.

It's just that I'm loving me.

I know what it's like not to love me,
not to value me.
Ain't going that route no mo'.

My Father done told me better
and I believe Him.

I am fierce.
I am woman.
That's me.

This was the Lord's doing; It is marvelous in our eyes.
Psalm 118:23

You are Man, You Are Beautiful

You are Man.
You are Beautiful.

Before you were formed in your mother's womb,
God knew you.

You were planned
and thought out.
Created in His image and likeness.
God's masterpiece.
His original design.

From your eyes,
to your hands,
to your feet -
even to the places on your body
you consider incomplete...

To the way you get your swag on -
Yeah, you know how to move.
To the way you talk -
You know how to say what you say.

To your mesmerizing smile -
Yeah, that smile...

That's what's up!

My brother, God's loving you
and you're loving you too.
Ain't nothing wrong with that.

How can you love someone else
if you don't love yourself back?

I can see by the way you carry yourself -
you know your value.
Yeah, you know your worth.

God validates and affirms you, man of God.
You're strong,
yet gentle enough to show compassion.
You're passionate,
yet temperate -
still having self-control.

Humbly serving God and His people...

You are Man.
You are Beautiful.

Living in pursuit of God's purpose -
No bugs are stopping you on the road to destiny.
I see your transformation.

I see your determination.
I see your stance for righteousness.
I see you being light and salt in the earth.

I see you standing on God's Word,
having faith and taking courage when others fear.

Go ahead, my brother, with your bad self!
Keep praising.
Keep worshipping.
Celebrate what God is doing in and for you,
even if no one else joins in with you.

Don't worry about your naysayers -
they just drinking on that hatorade... LOL.

They can't undo the plan of God,
nor stop the favor and oil
from flowing in your life.
Look up and continue to rise above.

You are who God says you are.
You can do what God says you can do.

Yes, you can.

You are Man.
You are Beautiful.

He has made everything beautiful in its time. Also He has put eternity in their hearts, except that no one can find out the work that God does from beginning to end.

Ecclesiastes 3:11

REFLECTION

Epilogue

ONE DOOR HAS CLOSED, ANOTHER HAS OPENED

> I know your works. See, I have set before you an open door, and no one can shut it; for you have a little strength, have kept My word, and have not denied My name.
> *Revelations 3:8*

Thank God for new beginnings!

In my journey to wholeness, I had to decide whether to continue mourning a closed door or embrace the new beginning. At some point, we will all come to this crossroads and have to choose: hold on to the past or let go and embrace our present and future.

The closing of one door in your life doesn't mean your life is over. It simply concludes a chapter in your history. There are still more chapters to experience in your book.

Don't be so engrossed in the past that you miss out on what God has for you right now. Refuse to be held hostage by regrets and fears. Your future doesn't have to be a repeat of your past. Take the lessons learned and walk confidently through your open door.

On the other hand, don't become stagnant with thoughts of the "good old days" either. There are more days ahead in which to do and experience good. You still have a life to live. Embrace your open door.

"I Hope You Dance" was written for my mother. After working 34 years for one company, she finally retired. That chapter in her life had closed, and a new one was beginning. This poem was my way of saying to her:

"Embrace this new beginning - your open door."

I took this to heart for myself too.

Although this piece was penned for her, I encourage you to insert your name wherever you see "Mama." Make this personal for you. And dance the dance that God has choreographed just for you.

**Everything that ended.
Everything I mourned.
Everything I lost...**

It wasn't the end for me.

On the contrary, it was the start of my new beginning - another open door.

I Hope You Dance

We all have our own unique dance to dance -
a life that God has ordered for each of us.

We can either embrace it or reject it.
We can either dance out the steps
that God has choreographed,
or make up our own along the way.

Mama, you've chosen the good part
- to follow God.
To dance His dance.

And there are yet:
more steps to be taken,
more words to be spoken,
more adventures to be explored,
more dreams to be fulfilled,
more promises to be made manifest…

So dance, Mama!

Go ahead and live life to the fullest.
Don't live inside the box.
Live - for with God,
there is no box.

Take the limits off
and embrace every new opportunity
that God presents with childlike faith.

Live a life that is free,
full of movement,
and completely saturated
in the Presence of God.

Rejoice!
Go ahead - Dance, Mama, Dance!

Be you.
Be different.

Laugh a lot.
Love much.

Enjoy your journey.
Dance your dance.

Whether on beat or off beat,
in rhythm or out of rhythm,
in time or out of time -
it really doesn't matter,
as long as you are in God's time.

Dance.
Live.
Dance, Mama!

Live your life…
no matter the situation.

When it looks like -
Dance still. Live still.

When it seems as if -
Dance the more. Live the more.

And when you feel as if -
Just dance, Mama. Dance!

Stand proud.
Stand firm.
Stand assured -
For God is with you!

This is your hour.
This is your time.

Seize it.
Savor it.
Bask in it.

One door has closed,
but another has opened.

The best is yet to come.
The latter is far greater than the former.
Go ahead, Mama -
Dance, dance, dance!

You turned my wailing into dancing; you removed my sackcloth and clothed me with joy, that my heart may sing your praises and not be silent. Lord my God, I will praise you forever.
Psalm 30:11-12

REFLECTION

But as it is written: "Eye has not seen, nor ear heard, Nor have entered into the heart of man the things which God has prepared for those who love Him."

I Corinthians 2:9

CONTACT AUTHOR

We'd Love to Hear from You

If *Reflections from My Heart* has blessed or inspired you in any way, we invite you to share your testimony. Your story could be the encouragement someone else needs on their journey.

You can follow Lanetta Allen on social media or connect with her through her author page at:

Because There's More Publishing
Scan the QR code or visit:
becausetheresmorepublishing.com

More books are on the way! Stay connected for future releases, updates, and inspiring content from Lanetta Allen and BTMP.

www.ingramcontent.com/pod-product-compliance
Lightning Source LLC
Chambersburg PA
CBHW070501100426
42743CB00010B/1709